Understanding My Muslim Neighbour

Some questions and answers

Michael Nazir-Ali is the Bishop of Rochester. He has worked in Pakistan as both priest and bishop. He also knows many others parts of the Muslim world well, and has a special interest in the Christian communities living in these areas. Bishop Michael has written extensively about Christian-Muslim dialogue.

Canon Christopher Stone is Director of Communications for the Diocese of Rochester and Adviser to the Diocese of Canterbury. Before taking up his present role in 1996, he was a programme maker and manager with the BBC.

Understanding My Muslim Neighbour

Some questions and answers

Michael Nazir-Ali
with
Christopher Stone

CANTERBURY
PRESS
Norwich

First published in 2002 by the Canterbury Press Norwich
(a publishing imprint of Hymns Ancient & Modern Limited,
a registered charity)
St Mary's Works, St Mary's Plain,
Norwich, Norfolk, NR3 3BH

www.scm-canterburypress.co.uk

British Library Cataloguing in Publication data

A catalogue record for this book is available
from the British Library

ISBN 1-85311-506-1

Typeset by Regent Typesetting, London
Printed in Great Britain by CPD (Wales), Ebbw Vale

Contents

Preface vii

Part 1: The Muslim Faith 1

The origins of Islam 1
Key Islamic beliefs 5
Allah 7
The *Quran* 9
Islam and other faiths 13
Conflict and violence 16
Prayer 20
Pilgrimage 23
The succession 24
Sunni, Shiite and Sufi 26
The spread of Islam 30
Conflict with Christendom 35
Islamic law 40
The heritage of Islam 44

Part 2: Islam Today 46

Al-Qa^c^eda and the Taliban 46
What it means to be a Muslim 51
Women and marriage 57
Interpreting the *Quran* 61
Fundamentalism 64
11 September 2001 70
Islamophobia 72
Get to know your Muslim neighbour 79

Part 3: Looking to the Future 86
Prospects for peace 86
Reciprocity 89
Terrorism 91
Optimism or pessimism? 96

Glossary of Terms 98
Further Reading 102

Preface

As a Christian, I have often found myself among Muslims. They have been fellow students, friends and relatives. A result of such close encounters has, naturally, been to try and understand their faith – the wellspring of their life, thoughts and actions.

I have written in greater detail elsewhere but this slim volume seeks, with the help of Chris Stone's pointed questions (shown in bold type), to understand Muslims and Islam in the light of recent international events. This is not a systematic treatment of Islamic belief and practice (though the Further Reading section at the end of the book may prove helpful in this respect). It is, rather, an 'impressionistic' account of Islam and Muslims in today's shrinking and fast-changing world.

It should, however, also be a look at ourselves and an opportunity to ask questions about our own awareness and willingness to reach out to what may seem unfamiliar or even threatening. Such a reaching out can result in dialogue about how each partner looks at the world and whether common values can be identified, even if we arrive at them from different starting points. From this, it may be possible to agree a common agenda for peacemaking and community development.

I remain committed to seeking an understanding of Islam and Muslims, particularly in terms of how their faith helps them to come to terms with the modern world. It is only in this way that the world of Islam will truly be understood as providing its own sources for an authentic engagement with contemporary opportunities and problems.

+Michael Nazir-Ali
Summer 2002

Part 1: The Muslim Faith

The origins of Islam

We begin with the origins of Islam. When? Where? How? But first, what does the word 'Islam' mean?

The word 'Islam' has a special meaning. It means 'surrender' – surrender to God. Some Muslims say that 'Islam' can also mean 'peace', and it is true that the root for 'Islam' and the root for the word 'peace' in Arabic, *Salam* or *Salama*, are the same.

As far as the origins of Islam are concerned, many Muslims would say that Islam is the eternal religion. By that, they mean that wherever people have worshipped the one true God, they have been Muslims, whether they have known it or not. According to them, the biblical prophets were Muslims, Jesus was a Muslim, and the disciples of Jesus were Muslims because they were all sincere worshippers of God.

Historically, however, the faith of Islam arose in sixth- and seventh-century Arabia, in the city of Mecca, the hometown of Muhammed, the Prophet of Islam. He belonged to a trading tribe called the *Quraish* and he was much influenced by Christians and Jews, but also by a group of sincere religious seekers in Arabia called the *Hanifs*. It was at the age of forty that he felt he had a particular calling to preach the message of the one true God and of God's guidance for people, particularly in the Arabic language.

How was his message received in Mecca?

Not favourably. He was preaching the one true God and Mecca was at that time a centre for the cult of the so-called 'Daughters of Allah'. You see, Allah is not an invention of the Prophet of Islam. Allah was the supreme high God even before the time of Islam, and the 'pagan' Arabs thought that Allah had three daughters, Allat, Al Manat and Al Uzza. Mecca was the centre of their cult, so naturally the preaching of Allah as the only true God threatened this cult, and that was the reason for opposition to Muhammed. In a Christian context, this reminds us of the opposition St Paul faced when he went to Ephesus, where his preaching seemed to challenge the cult of Artemis or Diana of the Ephesians.

And so what was Muhammed's response to this?

Eventually, though not immediately, he went to Medina, also in modern-day Saudi Arabia. When opposition first arose in Mecca, he sent his followers to Africa, to seek refuge in the Christian kingdom of Abyssinia, although Muhammed himself stayed behind in Mecca. These followers were well received by the Christian ruler, the Negus of Abyssinia, on the basis of a theological dialogue. The Negus asked them what they believed, and particularly what they believed about Jesus and the Blessed Virgin Mary. They said they believed Jesus had been born of a virgin mother and that Jesus was the word and spirit of God, and on that basis they were given refuge in Ethiopia or Abyssinia, which was then a huge empire. Some of them returned, but others never came back from there.

Eventually, the Prophet of Islam decided to leave Mecca. He had developed friendships in Medina, and these friends, who are called the *Ansar* or the helpers, assisted Muhammed in his migration from Mecca to Medina (originally known as Yathrib, the city was renamed Medinat-un-Nabi, 'city of the Prophet', in honour of Muhammed's arrival). This migration is itself of huge symbolic importance in Islam because it is the time from which the Islamic calendar is dated. Those who accompanied him to Mecca are known as the *Al-Muhajirūn.*

Once Muhammed had arrived in Medina, in due course, through negotiation and alliances, he became the temporal ruler of Medina as well as the spiritual leader of Muslims.

What about Muhammed's life: how far would you describe it as conventional? Was he himself a great scholar? A family man?

Well, it was conventional in terms of seventh-century Arabia. There were very few people then who were learned, in the sense of being learned in the scriptures of the Jews and the Christians, though Muhammed did know some such people. As far as his marriages are concerned, his first marriage to a woman older than him – Khadijah – who had also been his employer, was monogamous as long as she lived, and this has led some people to speculate that she may have had a Christian background. Certainly, Khadijah had Christian relatives, one of whom, Waraqa bin Naufal, was quite influential in the life of the Prophet of Islam. In those days, many people who were leaders contracted marriages to cement alliances, and at least some of the Prophet of Islam's other marriages were for that reason.

Key Islamic beliefs

What are some of the key beliefs of Islam?

The earliest preaching of the Prophet of Islam was very much to bring people back to belief in the oneness of God. The name he used for God was Allah, because that was a name already familiar to his Arab audience. He preached the need for repentance from idolatry and from other practices of the Arabs at that time, such as the killing of female children. Much of their time was wasted in drinking and gambling, and so a lot of Muhammed's preaching was an exhortation for people to change their ways. In that sense the earliest preaching is very like some of the preaching of the Old Testament prophets that we know.

Later on, when Muhammed had become the temporal ruler of Medina, the tenor of the teaching begins to change and there is much more detailed legal material in the parts of the *Quran* that were written there. There is also much more commentary on political affairs and much more reflection on relations with other people. All in all, the basic beliefs have to do with the oneness of God and with God sending prophets to guide his people – and, in this connection, many of the biblical prophets are mentioned, but also others who are not known from the Bible, such as Hud and Shu^{c}aib. Finally, God has sent Muhammed to the Arab people because they did not have the scripture in their language and he has now sent somebody who speaks in clear Arabic as a messenger for them.

Turning from the beliefs themselves to the practices which arise from those beliefs, there are what are known as 'The Five Pillars of Islam'. First of all there is the *Shahadah* – the profession of belief that there is no God but Allah and that Muhammed is the Prophet or apostle of God. There is then the *Salat* or ritual prayer, five times a day, which is very similar to the practice of the Jewish and Christian people around Arabia at that time. The third pillar is the practice of fasting during the month of *Ramadan*, which is called *Saum*. Next, there is the need to make a pilgrimage – the greater pilgrimage, the *Haj*, and the lesser pilgrimage, the *ᶜUmra*. (This was a practice that existed before Muhammed's preaching began but which was made Islamic in the course of Muhammed's work.) Finally, there is alms-giving, or *Zakat*, a word of Hebrew origin which is closely related to piety, so alms-giving arises out of piety.

Allah

Is the Allah of Islam the same as the God worshipped by Christians?

'Allah' is a pre-Islamic term for the Supreme Being. The Prophet of Islam used it to propagate his monotheistic message. It is also, of course, the ordinary name for God used by 15 million Arabic-speaking Christians. Islam explicitly claims continuity with the Judaeo-Christian tradition, even though there are significant differences between Christians and Muslims in their understanding of God. While Islam accepts Jesus as 'word' and 'spirit' of God, it cannot accept the doctrine of the Trinity which teaches the oneness of God with his Word and Spirit. We can, perhaps, sum up by saying that Islam refers to the Supreme Being worshipped by Jews and Christians but has a somewhat different understanding of such a Being.

Jesus is revered as prophet and messenger. His Virgin Birth, his miracles and some of his teachings are mentioned in the *Quran*. His glorification is also taught but the evidence is much more mixed about his suffering, death and resurrection. Although there are some indications of an awareness of atonement, generally speaking it is denied.

The Quran

The *Quran* is the holy book of Islam. How did it come to be written?

The word *Quran* is related to words like *qeryana* in Christian Syriac, which means 'reading' or 'recitation', and the word *Quran* relates to the original revelation to Muhammed, which was 'read in the name of the Lord'. That means that the *Quran* is, from the Muslim point of view, not only a book, but something which comes from God, which has to be recited, and that is still true for Muslims – the *Quran* is first of all memorizing and recitation.

I remember a well-known Muslim scholar saying to me that before the *Quran* is on the page it has to be in the heart and on the tongue, and because Muhammed is thought to have been illiterate, it was regarded even more as a miracle that he could recite the *Quran* in this way. There are various traditions about how, in his lifetime, what he was reciting was written down by scribes. All of this was collated after Muhammed's death in the reign of the first three Caliphs and standardized, and that is how the *Quran* became a book divided up into *Suras*, or chapters, and *Ayahs*, or verses. In fact, the word *Ayah* means 'a sign'.

And so, in the eyes of Islam, Muhammed was the last of the line of prophets, from Abraham to Christ himself?

In Arabic, he is called *Khatm an-Nubuwaa*, which means 'the Seal on Prophecy', and some people say that he is, indeed, the last of the prophets. The term itself, though, refers to the fact that he defines prophethood. In other words, they say, if you're looking for a definition of what a Prophet is or who a Prophet is, then look at Muhammed.

Muhammed is not himself divine then, though the words of the *Quran* are the inspired word of God?

That's correct. There is no claim in classical Islam for Muhammed being divine, though, later on, in popular Islam, many honours and titles were accorded him. For instance, he can be called 'saviour' or 'spirit of God', and many of the names given in popular devotional Islam to God like 'the merciful', 'the compassionate', and so forth, can be given to

Muhammed but without the definite article. So if God is *Ar-Rahim* – 'the merciful', 'the compassionate' – then Muhammed is simply *Rahim.* (There are, in fact, ninety-nine names for God in the *Quran* – the so-called 'ninety-nine beautiful names' – and the *Suras* often begin with an invocation to God.)

What, then, are the key messages of the *Quran*?

The *Quran* is roughly the size of the New Testament, with 114 *Suras*, and the earliest parts are about the one God, with exhortations to renounce idolatry, to live a virtuous life, to treat people justly, to give the weak their rights, and so on. Later on, there is much more guidance about how the Muslim community should live, about how it should conduct its relationships with others around, and about the Prophet of Islam's particular role in this community.

A whole chapter, for example, is devoted to reminding the Muslim community, as it is coming into being, of the guidance that God has given to the people of Israel in the past and of the guidance God has given through Jesus. There is a whole *Sura* on the status of women in society, and a *Sura* about what sorts of freedom there should be in a community –

how freedom is limited, for instance, and what kinds of punishment there should be for what are seen to be major crimes.

People often point to contradictions in the Bible. What about the *Quran*?

The Bible, of course, is a not a single book. Rather, it is a library of books and it was written over a very long period of time, in many different circumstances and cultural situations, and even in different languages, so if it says one thing in one context and something different in another, that's because of its very long history and diversity of circumstances. The *Quran* is very different in that sense, because it was completed in the lifetime of a person and collated within fewer than two generations.

That said, there are different views to be found within the *Quran*. There is the idea that a verse that occurs later in the *Quran* can repeal an earlier verse. If, for example, the *Quran* teaches friendship with a particular group of people and, later on, those people are found to be enemies of the Muslim community, and there is another verse that says you must be careful in your relationships with these people, then the later verse overrules the former. This is also true of food and drink. Food and drink that may be praised in one part is then forbidden in another because it has been found to be harmful. Such a view also applies to the earlier scriptures of the Jews and the Christians, and it is the *Quran* that is to be taken as definitive, even though the earlier scriptures are acknowledged as inspired.

Islam and other faiths

Let's turn now to what the *Quran* says about relationships with other faiths.

There is a whole range of views in the *Quran* about such relationships, particularly with Jews and Christians. These are the two faiths that are mentioned again and again and, at first, there is a sense of a common cause. The *Quran* explicitly says that Muslims do not believe in anything that has not been taught by the whole line of prophets, and it lists all the biblical prophets, Jesus and the tribes of

Israel (2:136). There's certainly a great deal about Jesus, about his birth, his miracles and his teaching. There are references to his suffering, to the Eucharist and to the apostles. Where commonality is concerned, Islam claims to stand in the same tradition from which Judaism and Christianity have come. Jews and Christians have not always accepted that argument. And yet, here are two other monotheistic religions and, surely, it was believed, the preaching of the Prophet will find a ready reception with them. That, however, turned out not to be the case and so the friendliness changes to suspicion and hostility. While the revelation to the Jews and the Christians is acknowledged, it is claimed that they have corrupted this revelation for their own ends, which is why they are not willing to receive the revelation that is now coming to the Prophet of Islam.

Certainly there seems to be agreement on a range of moral issues. No one would argue with the importance of giving alms.

Quite so. And, as I've already mentioned, the word for alms-giving, *Zakat*, comes from Jewish piety.

There are many other such verbal connections that can still be shown. Looking more widely, there are parallels in the need to worship only God, and in the people's experience of God's guidance, particularly his guidance of the people of Israel through the sending of Jesus, as the *Quran* has it. Even if they come to moral questions from different points of view, Christians, Muslims and Jews agree, to a very large extent, on the importance of family life, the dignity of the human person, and the need for justice in society.

Nonetheless, there is a tension between Islam and the two other Abrahamic faiths.

Yes, there is, and that tension is found not just in the *Quran* but also in the life of the Prophet of Islam himself. On the one hand, he clearly had a good knowledge of Christian and Jewish belief. Indeed, in Medina he attempted to arrive at an arrangement, particularly with the Jews, and he agreed treaties on a basis of equality with Christians. On the other hand, there is also conflict, both verbal and armed, and various kinds of warnings are issued to Jews and Christians, not only within Arabia but also to rulers in Christian lands surrounding Arabia – I'm thinking of the rulers in Egypt and the ruler of Byzantium – calling on them to accept Islam. It is true to say, however, that apart from certain skirmishes, the true expansion of Islam into those lands and beyond took place after the death of the Prophet of Islam.

Conflict and violence

I think the attitude of Islam to conflict and violence is something that is on many people's minds at the moment.

The *Quran* certainly teaches that those who are opposed to God must be opposed in turn by force of arms, and sometimes Jews and Christians are named among them. More often, though, they are the pagans – the *Mushrikūn* – those who associate other gods with Allah, the true God.

There are significant passages in the *Quran*, however, which suggest that faith should not be imposed on anybody, that there is no compulsion in religion and that, even with his pagan opponents, the Prophet of Islam sought an accommodation by which they would follow their faith and he would follow his (cf. 2:256; 109:6). The present debate in Islam focuses on where you put the emphasis and the weight. Do you put the stress on those passages that encourage you to try and arrive at an accommodation with the forces that are seen to oppose Islam or on those that advocate a confrontation with them?

Is this confrontation what is meant by *Jihad*?

Well, there are repeated exhortations to fight those who oppose the way of Allah, but the word *Jihad* comes from the root '*Jahada*' which simply means 'to strive', in the sense of striving to make Islam acceptable and to promote its spreading throughout the world. Muslim lawyers use a word derived from the same root, *Ijtihad*, which is all about striving to relate the law to present circumstances. The Sufis, who are those Muslims who seek close, direct and personal experience of God, use the word *Jihad* to speak of the internal struggle to control our base instincts so that we can give more of our time and energy to spiritual matters. However, *Jihad* can mean armed struggle to defend Islam or to protect the weak and powerless from harm.

Are there other holy books besides the *Quran* in Islam?

In the sense of revelation, Islam and the *Quran* itself acknowledge the Torah (what Christians call the Pentateuch or the first five books of the Bible) of the Jewish people. They acknowledge the Psalms of David and the Gospel of Jesus. Now, as I have said, this has to be seen as going hand in hand with the accusation that the Jews and Christians have corrupted their scriptures, though the *Quran* does not give any details about this. In later Islam, however, the debate has always been about whether the corruption is in speech, so you read the scriptures in such a way that people don't understand them, or whether it is a corruption in the text itself. The more moderate Muslims throughout history have seen it as using the scriptures in such a way that their meaning does not become clear, and the more hard-line element has taken it to mean that the Jews and Christians have actually altered the text. The Christian defence against this has always been that the mutual hostility of the Jews and Christians throughout history is the surest proof that this could not have happened.

In addition to these revealed books, there are six main collections of traditions about the Prophet of Islam, and these are used as a guide in formulating law. Indeed, they are the basis for Islamic law, or *sharīʿa*, and they are used also for inspiration and devotion for those who are trying to follow in Muhammed's way.

Prayer

Returning now to the Five Pillars of Islam, when we see pictures of mosques in the media, they often show people at prayer. You talked of the *Salat*.

Well, the ritual prayer, the *Salat*, consists of confession of God and of his Prophet, and of acknowledging God's sovereignty. Then there are certain passages of the *Quran* that are recited at different prayer times, but it has to be noted that, alongside the *Salat*, which is the ritual prayer, there is also *Dua*, which is extemporary prayer, and this can be prayed before or after the *Salat*, or at any other time.

And are these prayers at fixed times of day?

The *Salat* is fixed, yes. There is the prayer at dawn, the prayer at noon, the prayer in the afternoon, the prayer in the evening and the prayer at night. Interestingly, this bears a resemblance to Jewish practice, as well as to the Christian 'hours', the daily round of Christian prayer, still observed dutifully in some Christian traditions, and the basis for 'offices' such as Morning and Evening Prayer.

Each week, Friday is the holy day for Muslims, isn't it?

Yes. The word for Friday is *Jum^{c}a*, and the related word for a congregation is *Jama^{c}a*, so Friday is the day when Muslims are supposed to come together to pray. But while it is the day for congregational prayer, it is not considered a Sabbath in the sense of marking the day when God rested after the creation of the world. In the beginning, there was no demand for people to abstain from work and other activity – people would go to work, come to prayer, and go to work again. There was an emphasis on the close relationship between prayer and work. The 'Sabbatarian' Friday, which can nowadays be seen in some Muslim countries, is often an imitation of Jews and Christians, and is sometimes of secular inspiration.

Each year, *Ramadan* is one of the major Muslim festivals, and it's a time for fasting.

Indeed. *Ramadan*, however, is not only a month of fasting; it is also a time when the entire *Quran* is recited so that people are reminded of its message. It is a time for remembering the poor, and many people will undertake extra devotions, more than are actually required.

But there are many other festivals in Islam, just as in any other faith. The two main ones are the *Eid ul-Fitr*, which is the festival to celebrate the end of *Ramadan*, and the *Eid ul-Adha*, which is to celebrate Abraham's willingness to sacrifice his son. Incidentally, in the *Quran*, the son in the story of the sacrifice is not named, although in Islam, historically, it has been thought to have been Ishmael, Abraham's older son by Hagar, rather than Isaac.

Other festivals commemorate the finalization of the giving of the *Quran* to the Prophet of Islam, and the birthday of the Prophet of Islam, the *Eid Al-Milad un Nabi*, is becoming increasingly popular in Islam. Then there is *Muharram*, of which the first ten days are a solemn festival focusing on the martyrdom of the Prophet's grandson, Hussein, at Karbala.

This is observed particularly by the Shiite group, but it is a holy time for all Muslims.

Pilgrimage

And then there is the obligation to make a pilgrimage during your lifetime.

Pilgrimage, or *Haj*, is an obligation on every Muslim, if they can possibly undertake it financially. Because people from all over the world come together for *Haj*, it is a festival which reminds Islam of its universality. It is an icon of Islam's missionary nature and worldwide status.

The succession

We'll consider the question of universality later, but first I want to ask about the succession. Who succeeded the Prophet of Islam after he died?

Originally, there was a dispute about whether or not there should be any successor at all. In the end, it was decided that one of Muhammed's closest followers had been given a commission to continue, and that was the first Caliph, Abu Bakr. Haḍrat Umar, another close companion of Muhammed, followed him. His rule came to an end when he was fatally stabbed by a Christian slave, moved by the plight of those who had been taken captive during the Persian campaign. There was some question about whether the Prophet's nephew and son-in-law, Ali, should have succeeded Umar, but, in fact, it was Haḍrat Uthman, a more controversial choice for some. In the end, he too was murdered, this time slain by fellow Muslims. His actions are supposed to have resulted in a rebellion which ended in his assassination. Haḍrat Ali succeeded him, and Ali was killed as he came in for prayers, dying at the age of sixty after only five years as Caliph.

What does this word, 'Caliph', mean?

The word 'Caliph' comes from the Arabic word *Khalifah*, which means a viceroy or representative. In the *Quran* it is used generally of humanity. Humanity is the *Khalifah* of God on Earth (2:30) and, by extension, it is used of those who are now the representatives of the Prophet of Islam on Earth.

Gradually, when Islam became a very great empire, it assumed a political sense. The Caliph was the focal point for the unity of the empire, and that claim to have such a focus of unity, although it went through many ups and downs, survived until the twentieth century, when the Ottoman Caliphate was abolished in the 1920s.

Sunni, Shiite and Sufi

When we hear and see reports of Islam, there are often references to Sunni Muslims and to Shiite Muslims. What are the differences between them?

The ultimate authority for both lies in the *Quran* but, especially since the abolition of the Caliphate, Sunni Islam is focused more on the authority of the *Quran* and on how lawyers, theologians and scholars interpret that authority. For Shiite Islam there is always a focus of personal authority through which, and by whom, the *Quran* and the traditions of the Prophet of Islam are interpreted for life today. In that sense, if you want to use Christian terms, though these can be misleading, Sunni Islam is more 'Protestant' and Shiite Islam more 'Catholic'.

When Muhammed died, however, the succession was more complicated than it may seem at first sight. Some believed that Ali (although he became Caliph eventually) and not Abu Bakr should have been the first Caliph. These are the Shiite Muslims, and they have traced their authority through the line of Ali, stressing the importance of physical as well as spiritual descent from the Prophet. That is why those in every part of the world who are supposed to be descendants of the Prophet through Ali are very highly regarded. They are a kind of religious aristocracy in Islam, though materially they may be quite poor.

That way of thinking has focused Shiite Islam on the authority of a person, but there are different groups within Shiite Islam. In the main group, the *Ithna Asharia* ('the twelvers'), the twelfth Imam, or 'leader', disappeared in the ninth century AD. They are expecting his reappearance and, in the meantime, there are others who lead on behalf of the Imam. This is the kind of Shiite Islam that is the majority in Iran.

Then there are the *Ismailis*, of whom the *Aga Khanis* are a part, and the *Aga Khan* is their Imam, which is why he is given such honour. Finally, there is another, more moderate, Shiite group called the *Zaidi*, whose Imam was the ruler of the Yemen. So Shiism is not a monolith.

Some people say that 90% of Muslims are Sunni and 10% are Shiite. I would say that it is more 80% or 85% Sunni and 20% or 15% Shiite.

And then there's the third group, one you've already mentioned, the Sufis.

In fact, the Sufis can be found among both Sunni and Shiite Muslims. Sufism is a mystical movement in Islam rooted in parts of the *Quran* that speak of a personal experience of God's love, and speak of God as the light of the heaven and the earth (24:35). And so we find such thoughts as God's love for the righteous and their love for God (5:57). Sufism was also influenced, according to Muslim writers themselves, by the working ideals of the Christian monastic movement in Egypt and Syria. Indeed, the very word 'Sufi' comes from *suf* which means 'wool', the woollen garment that the monks wore and which many Sufis imitated.

Sufism became influenced by Neo-Platonism and, in some schools of Sufi thought, by Hinduism and Buddhism. It developed in a monistic direction. In other words, it held that all of reality was one. This can be seen in a story about Bayezid of Bistam, the famous Sufi whose disciples said to him once, 'Master, there must have been a time when there was only God and nothing else.' Bayezid said, 'Yes, and it's the same now!'

Alongside this monistic stream there was also a pantheistic stream in Sufism, which believed that God is everything and everything is God. Finally, there was a third stream which continued with orthodox Islamic belief but interpreted it in a very mystical way. Sometimes you find the same Sufi writer, such as Maulana Rumi, the founder of the Whirling Dervishes, writing for the orthodox in an orthodox way but writing for an inner circle in a monistic way. For example, he can say, 'I know no other but the one who is the sole existent!' and yet at other times he declares that, while a mystic can take on some divine attributes, he is like iron baking on the column of fire when it is heated. The fire does not make the iron lose its identity.

At the popular level, Sufism remains the religion of many Muslims, perhaps of the majority, and it is only when it has forcibly been rooted out, as in Saudi Arabia, that it has disappeared. Typical Sufi attitudes, at a devotional level, are seen in the anonymous Persian couplet:

People of God never become God
But they are never separated from God either.

The spread of Islam

How did Islam spread from its beginnings in Arabia?

It had already begun to spread through alliances with Arab tribes during the lifetime of the Prophet of Islam. Many of these tribes were nomadic and travelled all over that region. It was after the death of the Prophet of Islam, however, that Islam began to spread more widely when the Caliphs issued invitations to neighbouring rulers to accept Islam. If they declined, then Muslim armies, led by generals like Khalid Bin Walid and Tariq, went to war with those countries in the name of the Prophet. In many cases, the population and even their leaders capitulated peacefully. This was what happened when the Coptic Christian governor of Egypt surrendered Alexandria. In Damascus, the family of Mansour, the leading family, and the family of St John of Damascus, as he came to be later, opened the gates to the Muslim armies. And, in Jerusalem, the Patriarch Sophronius surrendered the city to Umar.

Very often, these Christian countries and cities were surrendered because it was thought that the Muslims would be better rulers than either the Persians or the Byzantines. People were tired of the incessant wars between Byzantium and Persia, and it was thought that the Muslims would bring peace.

A little later, Islam spread across North Africa, quickly subduing Roman North Africa, and crossed over to Gibraltar (*Jebel Al-Tariq* in Arabic, 'the rock of Tariq', the general who provided the bridgehead), through Spain and right up to the south of France, until it was stopped by Charles Martel. (It is worth remembering that Tariq was invited to cross over by certain Christian princes who were fighting against other Christians!) Islam also spread eastwards. The Persian Empire crumbled very quickly, and by the eighth century it had reached western India, now Pakistan.

But what about those people who refused to adopt Islam? How were they treated?

In the earliest days and, on occasion, during the lifetime of the Prophet of Islam, treaties were made with Christians, such as the Christians of Najran, on a basis of equality. Sometimes treaties were made, as with the Jews of the Khaibar, where the Jews had to pay a tribute in terms of crops, and so on, to the Muslims.

The constitution of Medina, which Muhammed promulgated after he became its temporal ruler, recognizes the rights of Christians and Jews in particular. When Islam spread outside Arabia, naturally the countries to which it spread, such as Egypt, Syria, Mesopotamia, Palestine, Roman North Africa and Spain, were wholly or mainly Christian countries and some also had sizeable Jewish communities. The new Muslim rulers depended on those mainly Christian and Jewish populations to continue economic and civic life and administration, because they did not have the means to do so.

What was devised, based on what the *Quran* says about Jews and Christians, was the system of the *Dhimma.* The word *Dhimma* means 'responsibility' or 'protection', and it meant that the Muslims were the protectors of the Jews and Christians, who at one time were the majority but later became minorities. In return for this protection the Jews and the Christians paid special taxes but, because they were often a conquered or a subdued people, they did not enjoy certain civic and political rights. They couldn't serve in the armed forces, and the highest levels of administration were denied to them; they could not marry Muslim women (though Muslim men could marry their women); they were not allowed to possess anything that might be used in military ways; they could not ride on horses; and their houses had to be more modest than those of the Muslims. As for their churches or synagogues, they could maintain them but could not substantially repair them, and they could not build new ones. All these were part of the system of the *Dhimma*, and it survived right up to the nineteenth century when, under Western pressure, the Ottomans abolished it.

When Islam spread to Persia and then to India, it had to examine the *Dhimma* system to see whether or not it could be extended to Zoroastrians, and even to Hindus and Buddhists. In due course this did happen and it became the way in which people of other faiths were organized under Islam and allowed to survive – sometimes tolerated, sometimes persecuted and sometimes able to make quite a significant contribution.

But very much as second-class citizens?

In political and civic terms they were, but they often made very notable contributions. In the building up of Islamic civilization, for instance, Christians often carried out the translation of philosophical, medical and scientific Greek works, either directly from Greek or from the Syriac into Arabic. The Muslims then took these, and commented on them, reflected on them and sometimes improved them. Incidentally, it was through this activity that the West received back, often through Jewish traders, many of Aristotle's works and much Greek medical knowledge. Quite often the typical physician in the Muslim world was also a Christian priest, and many Christians and others served in government, in architecture, and in many other essential walks of life, even if they were denied some important posts.

Conflict with Christendom

Thinking in particular of the Crusades, but also of other clashes over the centuries, Christianity and Islam have opposed one another. How do we begin to understand this violent past?

We must begin with the military expansion of Islam, though it's important to note that, in some cases, the spread of Islam, as on the Indian sub-continent, has been quite peaceful, through Sufi preaching and Sufi life. Islam has not always expanded militarily. Where it has sought to expand militarily, however, it has sometimes met with resistance. For example, there were centuries of armed incursions into Byzantium and it took Islam 800 years or so to conquer Constantinople. In Spain, in the end, the Muslims were pushed out, and the same with many of the countries of the Balkans, where the Ottoman Empire was gradually pushed back.

This has created a history of military encounter, and the Crusades are only one episode in that. We must not exclude the modern colonial movement, starting with Napoleon. One of the main reasons that triggered the Crusades was the activity of the aggressive Seljuk Turks who had only recently been converted to Islam. They blocked the way of pilgrims to the Holy Land and it was feared that Constantinople would also fall, leading to the Turkish invasion of Europe. That is not to justify all that happened in the Crusades, and the chivalry of Muslims like Salahuddin Ayubi (known as Saladin) can certainly be admired, though the aggressive way in which the recently converted Muslim Turks expanded into what remained of the Christian East should not be forgotten.

In colonial and post-colonial times there has been further armed conflict, and out of that came the dismemberment of the Ottoman Empire and the emergence of Arab nationalism once again. It's important to remember that the Arabs were ruled by the Turks for many centuries and that a renewed sense of Arab identity, to which Christians made a significant contribution, came out of that. In fact, it is arguable that without Western colonialism, without justifying it in any way, some of the independent Arab countries that now exist would not have come into existence.

You stressed earlier that Islam is not a monolith. Are there particular movements that have influenced the attitude of Islam to violence?

As with many other religions, there is always a tendency in Islam to go back to its roots, and it's almost a cyclical movement. By that, I mean that those who are going back to their roots today are looking back to eighteenth-century *Wahhabism*. In their turn, the *Wahhabis* in the eighteenth century were looking back to the thirteenth-century Ibn Taimiyya.

It's also true to say that different movements are inspired by different ideals. It's wrong to put them all into the same category. Take the case of *Wahhabism*, for instance. There has always been a tendency in Islam, represented by one school of law, which has seen utter fidelity to the *Quran* and to the practice of the Prophet of Islam as being more important than development in devotion, relation to circumstances and accommodation with other people. It is only one element, though, and out of four main schools of Sunni law, three find room for development, for new relationships and for adapting to new circumstances, but one school simply does not, and *Wahhabism* arises out of that tradition. It is not particularly focused on conflict, it is focused on purity, but that focus on purity leads to conflict. For instance, when the *Wahhabis* came to power in Saudi Arabia in 1926, after being used as an instrument by the Western powers against the Ottomans, the first thing they did was to destroy all Sufi and Shiite places of devotion. Naturally, this led to conflict with those who had valued those places of worship, devotion and memory, because some of them were tombs.

Like the *Wahhabis*, the *Deobandis*, in the Indian context before partition, focused on the same sort of purity. In the complicated story of the rise of what commentators now call militant Islam in the late twentieth century, there was a fusion of these movements.

On the other hand, as I say, these movements for purity are not typical of Islam as a whole. In India, for example, the *Barelvis*, the opposite movement to the *Deobandi*, were much more sympathetic to mystical Sufism as suiting the genius of Indian Islam.

Another group that also arose in pre-partition India, but is now worldwide, is the *Ahmadiyya* or the *Qadiani*, founded by Mirza Ghulam Ahmed of Qadian, who lived in the nineteenth and early twentieth centuries. At first, he was a reformist who wanted to renew the Muslims of the sub-continent, but he also claimed that he was the spirit of Muhammed as well as the Messiah reincarnate, and this led to many Muslims saying that he was denying the finality of Muhammed's prophethood. He therefore began to be regarded as unorthodox. There has been serious violence between his followers and orthodox Muslims for this reason and, in parts of the world such as Pakistan, they have formally been declared non-Muslim.

And so there is conflict and disagreement – violence even – within Islam itself.

Indeed, and some of the most serious violence taking place in parts of the Muslim world is between Muslims. It may be that their opinions differ or they come from different traditions. It also has to be pointed out that sometimes Islam has given birth to movements that are completely non-Muslim. The *Baha'i*, for instance, are a clear example of something that arose within Shiite Islam but has now become a movement that is not Muslim at all.

Islamic law

We've mentioned *Jihad* as an important concept and we will come back to that. Another concept I want to turn to now is *Shari^c^a,* Islamic law. How did that develop?

The word *Shari^c^a* means 'the way' and it arose out of a desire by Muslims to follow as closely as possible in the way of Muhammed. The codification of legal questions which arose in new settings depended, to a very great extent, on reliable traditions being passed on about what the Prophet had done in certain circumstances, how he had made political, family, and even economic decisions. It took two centuries or more for some of these traditions to be duly codified, and there are different schools of law in Islam that have certain differences in the way they understand the traditions and in the way they understand how *Shari^c^a* is to be applied.

Shari^c^a, then, became the legal system for the Islamic world, and as Muslims moved into other parts of the world it assimilated other legal systems with which it came into contact. For instance, as far as the treatment of people of other faiths is concerned, the Roman codes of Justinian and Theodosius were assimilated, to a very great extent, into the *Shari*ᶜ*a*. In the same way, the Persian way of dealing with communities on the basis of their faith became central to the *Shari*ᶜ*a*'s way of dealing with communities of Christians and Jews and others (more than just with individuals), and this was the so-called *Millet* system.

The Shiite developed their own code because they relied specifically on traditions about the Prophet of Islam which came through Ali, and not only through the other companions.

Eventually, it was decided that the codes of the four schools of law in Sunni Islam – the *Hanafi*, the *Maliki*, the *Shafi'i* and the *Hanbali* – were normative, and all that could be done in terms of collecting the traditions and reflecting on them had been done in their codification and use. This remained the case until these codifications began to be challenged under pressure from modern circumstances from about the eighteenth century onwards. That was when Muslim reformers like Sir Syed Ahmad Khan, Jamaludin Afghani and Muhammed Abduh in Egypt, Shah Wahiullah in Delhi, and Muhammed Iqbal, began to say that what was basic were the roots of law, which are the *Quran* and the *Sunnah*, and not the branches of the law as they have developed. They saw it as up to themselves to go back to the roots of Islamic law and to develop law according to their own circumstances, and that tradition continues. Many contemporary Islamic jurists point to the principles of movement that there have already been in some of the schools of law as a justification for developing further in this direction.

Nonetheless, *Shari^ca* has a bad name in the West, because it conjures up images of executions and of people losing their hands, for instance. How fair is this image?

It is a fair image of what some people think *Shari^ca* means, and it has been used in that way in the Arabian Peninsula, in Iran, Afghanistan, Pakistan and Northern Nigeria, for instance. But many Shiite jurists believe that while the crime which the *Quran* condemns, say of theft, is an absolute and that will always remain the case, the punishment for that crime can certainly take account of the tradition and the circumstances that prevail in a particular culture. So if a punishment was prescribed in seventh-century

Arabia because it was a desert situation, with no prison system and the like, it may not be an appropriate punishment in modern Iran. It is similar with marriage. If polygamy is permitted in certain circumstances, in other circumstances jurists may judge that monogamy is the best thing for the *Ummah*, the Islamic people. There have been powerful movements for the development of *Shari*^{c}*a* in this direction, some of them inspired by Sufism, which sees love as the supreme principle, and these movements have tried to interpret the *Shari*^{c}*a* in terms of love. As the poet Iqbal cries out:

I have not searched the highways and byways of
Shari^{c}*a*,
Except to know that it is denial of love which is the
true heresy!

The heritage of Islam

I want to end this first section by turning to the heritage of Islam, and to what Islam has given the world over the centuries.

It is difficult to generalize, because the Islamic world has included people from so many different backgrounds and has therefore produced a number of rich civilizations. If you take the Mogul civilization, for example, it brought values that come with a nomadic way of life – the values of hard work, of expansion, and of certain ways of understanding purity in life, for example. When Islam encountered the highly developed civilization of India, out of that mix came a unique Islamic civilization in terms of art, in terms of architecture, in terms of literature, in terms of dialogue with other faiths, and in terms of understanding Islam itself.

In Europe, perhaps Islam's greatest legacy is the way in which Greek thought, in its many different dimensions, was transmitted back to Europe and used in European universities for many centuries. Works from the Islamic medical corpus, for example, were still being used in the eighteenth century in Oxford as basic medical textbooks.

What we also have to understand in terms of culture and civilization is that the very things the Muslims received from Eastern Christians in terms of art and architecture and knowledge, they then developed in their own way and transmitted to others. That continual interaction, particularly between Christians and Muslims, has always fascinated me.

Indeed, the architecture and art of the south of Spain, for example, make up an amazing legacy.

It is amazing and it is only one legacy. Think of the Abbasid Caliphate, centred around Baghdad – that's another great legacy – and the way in which Muslim Persian culture developed is yet another. It all emphasizes the fact that there is no *one* monolithic Islamic civilization. Rather, there are a number of civilizations that arose because of the interaction of Islam with the local culture and tradition.

Part 2: Islam Today

Al-Qa^{c}eda and the Taliban

First of all, it's important to acknowledge that one of the reasons for this book is 11 September 2001 – and all that the events of that day are associated with. Two groups that instantly dominated the news, and continue to do so, were *Al-Qa^{c}eda* and the Taliban. What is the background to them?

Both *Al-Qa^{c}eda* and the Taliban are basically Sunni movements (see page 26), coming out of a particularly extreme understanding of *Wahhabi* Islam (see page 37) but almost veering towards *Kharijism.* The *Kharijites* form a movement on the margins of Islam that is strictly theocratic, allowing for no rule but that of God alone. That is one reason why secular rulers are afraid of them.

Theologically, the legal system that underpins them is the *Hanbali*, which does not concede any possibility of development in the understanding of Islamic law. That is why *Shariʿa* was applied very strictly when the Taliban were in power in Afghanistan.

The political reasons for their emergence as an international force have to do with what happened in Afghanistan and the surrounding area after the Soviet invasion of 1980. The West decided that there was enough resistance to the Soviet invasion and to the communist government there to turn Afghanistan into the Soviet 'Vietnam'. Through Pakistan, the Western powers, sometimes independently, encouraged a whole number of *Mujahidīn* movements. *Mujahidīn* is a word linked to *Jihad* and means 'those who wage *Jihad* against the aggressor'. *Mujahidīn* movements that emerged in Afghanistan were sometimes based across the border in Pakistan, and they had to be trained, so a whole number of training bases had to be created. The movements had to be armed, and so they were provided with arms. They had to be funded, so they were provided with funds. Once the pro-Soviet government in Afghanistan fell, the different *Mujahidīn* groups began to fight among themselves, and Pakistan and others saw the great danger of Afghanistan becoming 'Balkanized' and divided into different ethnic, or even religious, groups.

The Taliban arose as a movement of protest against this kind of Balkanization. The word 'Taliban' means 'students', and most of these people were students from the religious schools, the *madrassas*, mainly in Pakistan. They were supported by many because it was thought they would bring some integrity as well unity to Afghanistan. They were, however, from *madrassas* that were steeped in the kind of *Wahhabism* I have described, and they were unable to be flexible either with custom or with modern circumstances.

Alongside this indigenous movement to free Afghanistan, many other people from different countries who fought alongside the Afghans to free Afghanistan from Soviet influence also used the training camps. Eventually these people took the movement back to their lands, whether that was Egypt or Algeria or even Indonesia, and so the international movement has a point of origin which is political and geographical. It is inspired by the same ideals of Sunni fundamentalism and it has generally been anti-Shiite. Consider the fate of the Shi^{c}a after the Taliban took over in Afghanistan!

The international movement has fought against what it has believed to be compromise with the West and compromise with Israel. First in Egypt, and then in Algeria, it fought against old-style command-economy socialism. What has given it its motivation and passion, though, has been the existence of three or four flashpoints in the world. The main one is the Israel–Palestine question and the increasing Islamization of the Palestinian movement. The second is Kashmir because many of the people fighting for independence in Kashmir have been trained in the same training camps as the Taliban. Indeed, extremism in countries like Pakistan cannot be rooted out until the Kashmir question is settled. Among the other flashpoints are Bosnia, Kosova and now Chechnya. These are all related, and I think this has been seen as Judeo-Christian oppression of Islam and the need to free oneself from this oppression. It's been directed particularly against the United States because the United States is seen as the foremost supporter of Israel.

Incidentally, these movements in Sunni Islam are quite separate from the kind of Islamism that emerged in Shiite Islam in the Iranian revolution. That is also anti-American but that was because it saw American support for the Shah as oppressing the Irani people and, particularly, the Shiite divines. Now, of course, it also sees American support of Israel as another reason for its opposition.

As for *Al-Qa^{c}eda*?

Everything that I know of it suggests that it springs from a *Wahhabi* Sunni root, and Osama bin Laden himself comes from a Saudi Arabian family. It's also important to bear in mind that these movements are able to make alliances with one another. We shouldn't imagine them as in separate boxes. In the Middle East, for instance, I understand *Hizbullah*, which was fundamentally a movement in Shiite Lebanon, has links with Islamic groups in Palestine and, similarly, *Al-Qa^{c}eda* appears to have been given support by some Shi^{c}a in Iran.

What it means to be a Muslim

We'll return to this discussion of Islamic fundamentalism a little later. I want to consider now what it means to be a Muslim in the world today and to ask how we begin to understand our Muslim neighbours.

Islam is the fastest-growing religion in the world today and it now embraces some 20%, or even more, of the world's population. The number of Muslim majority countries has grown immensely, spreading from Morocco in the West to Indonesia in the East, and covering a huge area of the globe. That said, perhaps a quarter of the world's Muslims now live in minority situations where Islam is not the majority religion, including not only the West but also countries like India and, indeed, Israel.

The worldwide Muslim community is often referred to as the *Ummah*, which is a theological concept rather than a political one, though people are always trying to make it a political concept. Indeed, there are many pan-Islamic movements, including *Al-Qaᶜeda*, which want the whole of the Muslim world to be politically one again, possibly under a Caliph. Naturally enough, such an ambition comes up against the interests of nation states. Even with those who are not pan-Islamists in that extreme sense of the word, however, there is a sense of the Muslim world, or of a Muslim people, such that if Muslims are attacked in Afghanistan, Muslims in Britain can be grieved about it.

So while Islam is not monolithic, there is that sense of belonging. Earlier, you spoke about the Muslim discipline of prayer, and the importance that was attached to it as part of personal discipline. How much is that still the case?

It's certainly true in some parts of the world, such as the Arabian peninsula, where it is enforced and there isn't too much choice about it. As with other faiths, however, Muslims vary in their adherence to that faith and to the practice of that faith. There are many who will fast the whole month of *Ramadan*, for example, some will fast just for a few days and some not at all. Similarly, there are many who will pray five times a day, some who may try but not succeed, and some who won't even try.

How do Islamic communities organize themselves? Coming from a Christian background, we'd think in terms of the local congregation, the minister, and so on. Is there something similar?

Perhaps it's no surprise to discover that it varies from place to place and from time to time. In origin, however, the organization of the religious aspect of the community was led by the leader of that community, so leadership in prayer was always regarded in Islam as a sign of wider leadership in the community, and this still is the case in some parts of the world. That means that the *Imam* is not just the leader in prayer, but also the leader of the community. In parts of the world, and certainly in the West, these functions have become separated. The *Imam* is now somebody who leads the community principally in the mosque and who provides for rites of passage, for leadership in prayer, for the maintenance of the mosque and so on.

There is another official in Islam, and sometimes this office is combined with that of *Imam*. This is the *Khatib*, the person who is learned in the *Quran* and who teaches others the *Quran*, particularly its memorization, and who preaches. In addition, there will generally be a mosque committee that oversees the work of the mosque and, in some cases, selects the *Imam* and the *Khatib.*

Another word we often hear in this context is '*Mullah*'.

'*Mullah*' is a generic word, meaning a religious leader, and the *Imam* or the *Khatib* can be a *Mullah.* In fact, the word '*Mullah*' is used less now because it's come to have a derogatory sense and the word that may be used is *Maulvi*, meaning something like 'lord' or 'sir'. In some cases, alongside the mosque committee, there may be a welfare organization that looks after the social needs of the community attached to the mosque. There may also be a youth organization affiliated to the mosque. Sometimes a mosque can become the centre of political activities, even supporting a particular political party.

What role does the mosque play in terms of birth, marriage and death – those rites of passage?

Marriages generally happen in people's homes, and the circumcision of a boy or the *ʿaqiqa* of a girl will happen in the home. For a funeral, certainly of a man, there can be prayer at the mosque before the body is taken to the graveyard. In general terms, the mosque is used for prayers and perhaps for study, and it can be a place for public meetings. Beyond that, it is a place of hospitality for strangers, and food is often distributed from the mosque.

How are children introduced to the faith?

They may be taught at home or in the mosque, and there can be a *madrassa*, a school, attached to a mosque. Some *madrassas* are places where all of a child's education takes place, particularly if they are very poor, but many children will go to the mosque after their ordinary school day to learn the *Quran* and so forth, or somebody may come to their home.

Prayers are not confined to the mosque, are they?

Not at all. Most people would say their prayers at home, at school or college, or wherever they happen to be. Like fasting, prayer is something that can happen anywhere.

It's noticeable that the name of God is very often on the lips of the Muslim.

That may not be because they're Muslims but because they come from a culture that sees the spiritual as very much involved in the ordinary course of life. You may find Christians from Arab countries, for instance, talking like that, and in Africa you find Christians talking like that all the time. In this sense, Christians from Africa, Asia and Latin America may have more in common with Muslims than with some of their fellow Christians in the West!

Inside the mosque men and women are separated.

In some parts of the world, women do not or cannot go to mosques. In others they go to a separate part of the mosque and in still others they may go before or after the men.

Women and marriage

Forced marriage and arranged marriages are often mentioned in connection with Islam.

In Islam, marriage is a contract between a man and a woman, and is witnessed by certain prominent people in the community, including the *Imam*. Some schools of law, on the one hand, have said that it is a contract between a man and a woman that must be freely undertaken. Other schools have taken a different view, saying that a woman needs the permission of a *Wali*, or her protector, her parent or guardian, to enter such a contract.

There have been recent challenges in various Muslim courts about whether or not a woman had the permission of her *Wali* to marry somebody. Some courts have ruled that she does not need the protection or the permission of her *Wali* to marry and that women and men are equal in this respect under Islamic law, so that there can be freedom.

It is in connection with this practice of a woman having a *Wali* who is her protector and who must give permission for her to marry that the question of arranged marriages arises. In some Muslim countries women marry as they choose. In others, there are certainly arranged marriages, but arranged marriages are of many different kinds and they are not restricted to Muslims. They may affect non-Muslims living in that part of the world as well. An arranged marriage can be where a man and a woman know one another, and then tell their parents to arrange their marriage because they like one another. On the other hand, it could be the parents' initiative in introducing them, and the couple then signal their willingness to marry the person to whom they have been introduced. In the most extreme circumstances, it can be a marriage where the person hasn't even seen the other party, and this could be called a forced marriage, though not always. Sometimes people do agree to marry someone they haven't seen. It still remains, though, that there can be no marriage without consent in Islamic law, so if it is genuinely a forced marriage, then it is no marriage at all.

What about Islam's attitude to women more generally? In many eyes, for example, the *burqa*ᶜ may well seem oppressive.

It comes from a general Middle Eastern way of

assigning different roles to the different sexes. If you consider the habit of a nun, it comes from the same family as a *burqa*[c], and if you look at pictures of the Blessed Virgin Mary, she is usually wearing a *hijab*. It comes out of a culture where Christians, Jews and Muslims all had a certain way of dressing, men as well as women. The *burqa*[c] itself, covering the face, is not particularly Islamic. It is more Indo-Iranian and even now in places like Rajisthan, you see Hindu women wearing it. It has to do with things like shame, and the view among men that seeing the face of their women brings shame on them. Covering the head is an old Jewish idea, and the rabbis say that even the rafters of a ceiling in her house don't see the hair of a pious woman, and this was certainly the case with Christians. In the New Testament itself, to cover your head was a way of showing that you were a decent woman and not a prostitute (1 Corinthians 11:1–16).

But in Saudi Arabia, for example, I believe women are not allowed to drive a car.

That is a particular *Wahhabi* interpretation of Islam. Against that, it's important to understand that in early Islam, for example, the Prophet's first wife had been his employer. Then there are stories in the Islamic tradition of *ᶜA'isha*, one of the wives of the Prophet of Islam, who arrived on a camel to fight a battle. Equally, there have been women rulers in Islam.

What is true, though, is that Islam, like Christianity and Judaism, comes out of a largely patriarchal culture, and many Muslim women today are struggling to find their true place in Islam. Given the example of some Muslim women, certainly in the past, there is the possibility of development in Islamic societies.

Muslims will often point out that it was possible for Muslim women to hold property and to engage in business on their own before that was possible in the West. In some respects, then, Islamic women have been quite prominent, and women leaders have sometimes been acceptable in Sufism.

Interpreting the Quran

How important is the *Quran* today?

The *Quran* is as important as ever. The questions that are being asked today have to do with how the *Quran* has been understood in the past, particularly as a basis for law. Given the diversity in the *Quran* itself, they also ask whether or not there can be new understandings in relation to law, in relation to the place of women in society, in relation to non-Muslims, and in relation to questions about *Jihad*. On the one hand, while the text of the *Quran* is inviolable, on the other, people are certainly asking questions about how it is to be used in today's world.

With different answers in different places?

That goes without saying. Take *Jihad*, for instance: the most extreme people will answer the question about *Jihad* by saying that Muslims must treat all non-Muslim territory as the abode of war, ultimately to be subdued and conquered. Many other Muslims, perhaps the majority of them, will not take that view and will say that *Jihad* has to be understood first of all as an effort to remove social ills from society, as a way of subduing one's lower self or as a way of armed struggle when Islam itself is in danger. They won't go beyond that.

As for the position of women in society, some will say that the fundamental view of the *Quran* is that human beings, men and women, are all equal because they're made by God and made as his representatives. On the *Shari^ca*, many will say that the *Quran*'s teaching about not imposing one's faith on others is important in the treatment of non-Muslims in the Muslim world.

How the *Quran* is to be used is the important question. There are some scholars who have tried to understand the origins of the *Quran* in the literary sense, in terms of its relationship to the Bible, for example, or its relationship to the Arab culture in which it arose and so on. That work will go on and Muslims need to be reassured that it does not in any way call into question the integrity of the *Quran* but is an attempt to understand it better.

What about changes in belief?

In the sense that a monotheistic religion from the

desert was turned into a kind of religion that had achieving union with God as its basic element, Sufism was a huge shift in belief, though still rooted in the *Quran*. Movements like *Baha'ism* have moved right away from 'Islam' altogether. The *Qadianis* are another example of Islam relying very much on their own founder. So there have been many changes in belief, at least among certain groups. Also, like any other religion, Islam has evolved and has elaborated its theological system in different ways.

One particular change that needs to be noted is the way in which the person of the Prophet of Islam has been treated. The *Wahhabis* are very keen to emphasize that he was only a man and, in that sense, the Prophet is their brother. In some other traditions of Islam, however, there has been an attempt to understand the Prophet in an almost 'Christological' way as a saviour, as the presence of God, and as one who can be invoked. Some of the struggle within Sunni Islam is often about that sort of thing.

Can there be such a thing as a secular or a non-practising Muslim?

Very much so. There are many Muslims in many

parts of the world who are non-practising or who are very occasional attenders, even though they may fast or pray. And there are huge numbers in Asia where all their socialization, their names, their spiritual terminology, are pre-Islamic. Even the names of the Muslim festivals are pre-Islamic. That's another kind of nominalism.

Fundamentalism

Now we turn to another '-ism': fundamentalism. What does that term mean to you?

It is an unsatisfactory term, but it means something like the desire to go back to the roots of a faith, particularly to sacred texts. It's about a desire to interpret these texts in a very literal way, without giving enough attention to how a text arose in its original context and without giving enough attention to the present circumstances and context in which it has to be interpreted and applied.

And why is it a word we hear so much about today?

In fact, as I have been saying, there have been movements of this kind throughout Islamic history, and there have been different reasons for 'fundamentalism' at different times. In our own times, my view is that it has arisen in part because of the experience of colonialism. The experience of being colonized either by European powers directly or by the Ottomans made Muslims ask what it was that was fundamental about Islam that could guide them if they were to rule themselves. It's been more than a political motivation born out of the experience of colonialism, though. It's also the experience of what some people call neo-colonialism.

I have already mentioned the Russian invasion of Afghanistan in the 1980s, but to that can be added the way in which the Western powers handled the Suez Canal crisis in the mid 1950s, and became involved in the destabilization of governments such as that of Iran, for example, also in the 1950s. All these factors made some Muslims determined to make sure that their polity and even their economy is founded on Islamic principles so that they are not left exposed to hostile interference. From the economic point of view, the interest in economics based on Islamic principles has been fuelled by the experience of debt and by the failure of capitalism more generally in many parts of the Muslim world, where it made a few people rich but left the majority poor. As for the command economy of old-style socialism in countries like Syria and Egypt, that too came to be seen as a failure, as it made for gross corruption, inefficiency and bureaucracy.

So in some ways it's a reaction to forms of oppression?

Quite often it's been that, but sometimes it's been combined oppression and deprivation. The exploitation of people by their rulers or by the imperial powers, extortion of unjust revenues, and the extravagant lifestyle of the elite, all contributed to the reaction.

Where is Islamic fundamentalism continuing to make its presence felt, in your view?

It is becoming influential in Central Asia through Afghanistan and, to some extent, Iran. In Iran itself, of course, and to some extent with the Taliban in Afghanistan, revolutionary movements have been based very much on an Islamist fundamentalist reading. In addition, in some countries like those of the Arabian Gulf, it has been used to sustain the status quo, so the rulers have come to an accommodation with conservative movements to make sure that they survive.

Is that within both Shiite and Sunni traditions?

Yes, indeed.

But why is fundamentalism so often associated with *Jihad*, and what many people consider to be the suffering of the innocent?

It is being expressed in *Jihad* at this time because the aim is to get rid of those who are seen as oppressors of the Muslim world. In Afghanistan that meant the Soviet Union, whereas it was the United States of America in post-revolutionary Iran, and in the Middle East today it is Israel and all the friends of Israel.

What will the outcome be? What can be done to prevent another 11 September?

Sometimes things seem hopeless but, while I think people should remain concerned, there are certain things we should do. We should do all we can to make sure that the flashpoints in the Muslim world – the disputes in Israel and Palestine, Kashmir and Chechnya – are resolved in a way that is just. Secondly, it is important to encourage moderate Muslim opinion, supporting those who see Islam as a tolerant faith that is able to live alongside others, and that can create a polity and an economic system which is not oppressive, whether of Muslims or of non-Muslims. International co-operation against terrorism is very necessary and, to some extent, can be effective, but I think that what motivates fundamentalist groups is the continuation of what they see as injustices, and these have to be addressed.

Again, though, we have to remember that Islam is not a monolith and that not all Muslims share the same point of view on these issues. There are tensions within.

Indeed, and there are Muslims who would prefer secular states. Equally, though, I can think of states that are influenced and inspired by Islam which are both tolerant and able to live at ease in the modern world. What characterizes some extremist movements is their desire to coerce people, if necessary by force of arms, into a system which they believe to be right. That has to be resisted and must be actively discouraged wherever it occurs, and we have to be consistent in doing this. We can't say that it is wrong in one part of the world but in another, because, say, we have huge trade relations there, acquiesce in it.

But within Afghanistan, for example, both those Afghans who were fighting the Taliban and the Taliban themselves were Muslim people.

These things are never just religious movements: there are ethnic, linguistic and political elements to them. Afghanistan is divided among a huge number of ethnic groups and the struggle was not so much between fundamentalist and progressive, or whatever, but between the Persian-speaking Tajik people of the north and, to some extent, the Hazara and the Pashtun of the south.

There is an Afghan proverb which says that, after God had made all the other countries of the world, he had some bits left over and out of them he made Afghanistan. In other words, the country is a patchwork of ethnicities, religions and languages. There is always a potential for conflict in such a situation.

11 September 2001

How far can it be said that 11 September 2001 was a declaration of war by Islam on the West?

As a generalization, that simply does not hold. The most that can be said is that it was a declaration of war by a small, though powerful, Islamic movement against the West. They had done it before when they bombed the American Embassy in Nairobi and when they attacked the American warship in Yemen. It had happened on other occasions. This was, perhaps, the most dramatic instance, and they will continue to wage these acts of war as far as they are able to.

Such acts seem bound to colour the way in which people of different faiths relate to their Muslim neighbours. What can be done to rebuild bridges between the communities?

Well, yes, they are bound to colour relationships and that is an unfortunate fact, but we should work, wherever possible, to create a better understanding of Islam in its comprehensiveness. It then follows that if we are to build one world we have to find common values. Now, our reasons for holding those values may differ, but it is quite possible to encourage Muslims, for instance, to find the roots of tolerance within Islamic tradition itself.

Dialogue is important, then?

Dialogue is important but it is only one aspect of what I am talking about. Education is another aspect, for instance, as is support for those who are trying to control extremism in their own countries.

Islamophobia

Islamophobia or anti-Muslimism, is another of those terms we often hear today, particularly from those who are subjected to it. But it's not new, is it?

In one form or another it has been around for a very long time because Islam, both as polity and people, has been felt to threaten Western Europe for many centuries, and the fear of the Saracen during the Crusades and, later on, the fear of the Turk are well documented. More recently it has been fuelled by the increase in the numbers of Muslims from different parts of the world living in Europe. There is also a new and heightened awareness of indigenous European Islam – in the Balkans, for instance – and, of course, terrorist events have come to be associated with some Muslim organizations.

How would you define Islamophobia?

I see it as an unreasonable fear of all Muslims, without taking into account their beliefs, their direction in life and what tradition of Islam they come from. It is very important to distinguish that from a reasonable fear, for example, of people who are committed to terrorism to achieve their aims.

Away from the West, there is Islamophobia on other continents.

In India, for example, there is a very long history of Hindus and Muslims trying to live together in one vast land, and the creation of Pakistan and Bangladesh is a testimony to the desire of at least some not to continue living together. The problem is that India now has more Muslims than does Pakistan and so the question hasn't gone away. In India there are disputes, like the Kashmir dispute, which have brought Islamophobia to the fore, but there is also an element of extreme Hindu nationalism which sees people of any other faith as alien in India and wants to remove them, be they Muslims or Christians or from any other religion. That has been the reason for a lot of the violence that has taken place recently in Gujarat, in Western India.

What can be done to combat Islamophobia, then, here in the West, for example?

Some Islamophobia can be privately held opinion, and if people have opinions which they have not examined and given some time to see whether they are justified, that in itself can be very damaging. If these people are in decision-making positions in local authorities, or in large companies as employers, then it can result in discrimination against people because of their religion rather than their race or gender, and we are only on the threshold of recognizing the extent of discrimination on grounds of faith in this country.

Islamophobia can also be seen in more organized movements, and the ways in which anti-Muslim groups have pressurized areas in which Muslims live have led to counter-moves in the Muslim community. It has increased ghettoization in those communities. It has left them more exposed to influence from Muslim extremist groups, and it has polarized people in towns, particularly, but also in larger cities.

Another example of Islamophobia we have heard

of recently is the accusation, particularly in Europe, that 'peasant' Islam, as it has been called, is responsible for backward-looking practices and opinions. In fact, 'peasant' Islam all over the world is not extremist at all. It is very much mystically and devotionally inclined and has not, on the whole, taken any significant role in the more extreme movements, and so to lay the sins of the extremists at the door of 'peasant' Islam is very unjust.

Finally, misunderstandings that people have, and do not examine – about marriage practices, for instance, or inheritance laws, or diet, or patterns of prayer, or time needed for observing religious festivals – can lead to Islamophobia.

How can Islamophobia be overcome, then?

Education, education, education is the answer, and on both sides. The more people know about one another, the less unjustified fear there will be. Muslims, particularly where they are a minority, need to appreciate the traditions, the values and the history of the communities in which they are living, while the community as a whole needs to appreciate the diversity in Islam more, and the way in which different Muslims organize their personal, family and social lives.

Getting to know your neighbour, friendships at the workplace and in social contexts, are also very important. I was heartened to learn recently that many people in the United Kingdom, for example, now have someone from another ethnic background or faith in their immediate friendship group. There's nothing like friendship to reduce prejudice. It may be necessary, however, particularly to reassure Muslim and other religious communities, to have some legislative protection so that any offences against a person or against a place that have an element of religious prejudice in them are duly recognized by the courts.

I wonder if some people will say that this is bending over backwards to be accommodating?

This is why I say the process of education has to be mutual. When Muslims are in a particular community, they need to understand that they should recognize the way in which that community understands itself in terms of its history, its faith, the values it has and its direction for the future. At the same time, communities also need to understand the great diversity of Muslims in many countries. They come from many different backgrounds and they have many different educational attainments. While some of them want to assimilate, others do not, and questions need to be asked about the extent to which integration should be encouraged and the extent to which people should be allowed to celebrate their culture.

You could have a community like the Hasidic Jews who do keep themselves to themselves but also make a contribution to the community and certainly do not cause any disruption in a community. That may also be the case for some communities of Muslims who, because of their piety, their religious observance and their social customs, keep themselves to themselves because that is how their community works. The key thing is for them to recognize, and for society to recognize, that there must be a level of interaction. I'm thinking, for example, of the need to speak a common language so that misunderstandings can be removed, so that there can be a common programme for development, and so that educational and medical needs can be adequately met.

What role do you see for an organization like the United Nations in working for understanding between Muslims and others?

In recent years, the UN has become more and more conscious of the religious and spiritual dimension to national and regional life and also to international conflict and, indeed, conflict within nations. They now have a unit which encourages dialogue between people of different faiths, not simply to understand one another, but to co-operate, for example, on particular economic programmes and on questions to do with human rights and responsibilities. This is also true of other international organizations, such as the World Bank.

Nonetheless, it so often seems that the voice of moderation, on both sides, fails to be heard.

Yes. There is the story of a student at Harvard who wanted to give his fellow students the proper view of *Jihad*, as a Muslim, but he was condemned before he was heard because everybody thought they knew what *Jihad* was. It is certainly true that the moderate Muslim voice has not been heard enough in recent years, and when there has been conversation between Christians and Muslims the moderate voice has been drowned out by other voices.

One of the positive things coming from the great evil of 11 September has been that moderate Muslim voices in all parts of the world *are* being heard. They are clearly condemning terrorism, clearly saying that the taking of innocent lives is no part of genuine Islam, trying to point out that there is a diversity of views in Islam about *Jihad*, for instance, and wanting to be in dialogue with Christians and others about when conflict may be justifiable.

Get to know your Muslim neighbour

So, if I want to do something positive in terms of my own commitment to understanding my Muslim neighbour, where do I begin?

The first thing is to get to know your neighbour, not to be put off by differences in dress or diet, or by the ways in which families live. There was a fire in a Muslim home recently and some members of that family were killed. It was very moving to see a mother from a different ethnic group with a little child going to lay flowers on the doorstep of the house, showing human fellow feeling and sympathy for other people's sorrows and joys. That is certainly the place to start, but then it is important to go on in terms of getting to know what people believe, to know their background and what it is that makes them tick. It's also important to encourage them to learn about your own background and the community from which you come, to join together in activities that are for the common good, in a particular street, town or village. I heard of the mothers of young people in a town where there was to be a huge shopping centre, getting together from different faith backgrounds to engage in dialogue with the employers in their area about opportunities for their children. That is the sort of constructive action that leads to widespread respect for faith in the community, and also leads to greater friendship, a common purpose and the sort of dialogue that is good for a community.

And yet, both Christianity and Islam are missionary religions. Is there a way in which a Muslim can

be 'saved', in a way that a Christian would understand, without a conversion experience?

We must remember that salvation is from God and this salvation is definitively declared in Jesus Christ. God's Holy Spirit is working to convince men and women everywhere of their need for salvation (John 16.7–11) and the Eternal Word, incarnate in Christ, seeks to bring divine illumination to all (John 1.9). The great evangelical Christian, Sir Norman Anderson, who was also a scholar of Islam, recognized that there were some in the Muslim world who had experienced brokenness, repentance and a sense of utter dependence on God. He believed that Christ's work would be made effective for them, either through Christian mission or through God's providence in some other way.

So should my stance be one of wanting to convert my Muslim neighbours to Christianity while, at the same time, expecting them to be encouraging me to convert to Islam?

From the Christian point of view, our task is to witness to what God has done for us in Christ. We must do that as clearly and effectively as we can. It is the work of God, the Holy Spirit, to convert people and we believe that the Holy Spirit is working in people's lives and in the world to convert people of all kinds to God's purposes for them. Similarly, with Islam, the concept of *Da*[c]*wah* is of an invitation from God to turn away from idolatry and sin to God.

Neither Christians nor Muslims can take the place that properly belongs to God, but Islam and Christianity are both missionary religions with a message to proclaim and a way of life to live. I have found, in my own experience, that the best way for them to live together is to acknowledge that they are both missionary religions. If Christians deny that there is a missionary aspect to Christianity, that is dishonest and will not be believed anyway. Similarly, we know that the desire of Muslims is for other people to accept Islam. Provided there is honesty about that, I don't see why that witness itself cannot be a basis for continuing dialogue.

When I was Bishop of Raiwind – the largest Islamic missionary society is based there – that is how we related to one another. They came to us, we went to them. We were clear about the good news that comes to us in Jesus and, in the end, they wanted to invite us to accept Islam as a way of obedience to God. These are both honourable things to desire. There's nothing wrong with a desire that people should share our beliefs and we need, with patience, to listen to one another, as well as to give an account of the faith that governs the whole of our lives. That is what we did and, because there was willingness on each side, we had reasonably good relations while maintaining the integrity of each faith.

The same would be true of interfaith groups, where people not only from Islam and Christianity but from a range of different faiths work together on a project of mutual concern, learning about one another and, at the same time, producing something that is agreed between them all.

I have just given the example of the mothers who came together around the issue of employment opportunities for their children. Similarly, other interfaith groups may have other kinds of agenda. For instance, they may want to participate as communities in the regeneration of their neighbourhood, for which the Government may provide some of the money, or they may want to make sure that patients in hospital in their area have access to spiritual care from the faith community to which they belong. There are all sorts of reasons for interfaith groups to come into existence and for them to flourish. Of course, they are also a place where people share their faith, listen to one another and talk to one another, and that deepens their knowledge and their experience.

What about interfaith worship? That's something that both Christians and Muslims can find quite a difficult issue.

I had a dinner some time ago for representatives of different faiths. A commercial organization had offered a space that they said must be available to people of all faiths and we were considering how we might use it. It was interesting that all the representatives of faiths of Indian origin, like Hinduism, Sikhism, Buddhism, and so forth, were quite happy about everybody worshipping together in the same place, but the Jews, Christians and Muslims were much more reserved in their position. That showed me that there is a big divide here. For Christians, of course, worship is Christ-centred and that makes for difficulty with interfaith worship. As for Muslims and Jews, they would find it difficult to worship anywhere where there was a cross or other symbols of the Christian faith.

Interfaith worship can never be part of the ordinary spiritual diet of Christians because, without Christ being at the centre, Christian worship is emptied of a great deal, if not all, of its meaning. There are some occasions, however, when prayer with a person of another faith, or some remembrance, or celebration together, may be necessary. I've often been in situations where a person of another faith has asked me to pray with them and I've always done so. Quite often, on national occasions or international occasions, a Christian will be asked to read or to pray or to say something, and it is good to take the opportunity without offending other people. When there is a national disaster or a local disaster or, indeed, a time of great celebration, it may be necessary for Christians to join with others in a simple act of remembrance or of celebration. Sometimes, just being quiet together or listening to one another, without necessarily taking part in what the other is doing, is enough.

Part 3: Looking to the Future

Prospects for peace

We're turning now to look to the future. What are the prospects for peace between Islam and the West? Or is that too big a question?

I have to say that categories like 'Islam' and 'the West' are too monolithic. It really is not as if Islam is out there and the West is here. There are, in fact, significant Muslim communities in the Western world. Some have arrived from other parts of the world and some are indigenous. Even among those who have arrived from elsewhere, they are now into their second or third generation. With many Muslims, there is a desire to be able to live according to their faith and to practise their faith in freedom. This can lead to Christians pointing out that other people, including Christians, also desire what Muslims desire for themselves, and so the idea of reciprocity is very important for the future. I don't mean 'tit for tat', with Muslims having freedom in the West only if they provide similar freedoms in the Muslim world. I do think that one element in our dialogue, however, must be a common commitment to basic human freedoms throughout the world, respect for fundamental rights and an acknowledgement of our responsibility – that's the word *Dhimma* again – for those who have less power or less economic strength than we do.

There has been much fruitful interaction between Islam and other faiths in the past. Earlier in this book, I mentioned the example of Mogul India, where a new civilization was produced because of the interaction of different groups. Classical Islamic civilization developed because of the contribution of Christians and Jews, and, in turn, it contributed to the Renaissance in Western Europe. There is no reason why, in our age of increased communications, such exchanges should not continue to occur. In fact, they should occur at an accelerated pace.

Yet it is undeniable that, in some parts of the Islamic world, we need to see some quite basic changes, some acknowledgement of representative government, and the fuller participation of women in the political process. In Pakistan, for instance, 33% of local authority seats in recent elections were reserved for women and that means that every local authority chamber at every level will have a third of its representatives being female. I'm sure that in ten years or so that will bring a huge change to the agenda of local authorities. Women's concerns and the concerns of children will be much more to the fore.

Discriminatory laws that curb the freedom of non-Muslims have to go. There is no place in the future for blasphemy laws, such as those in Pakistan, which threaten death for anyone who is accused of saying anything against Islam or the Prophet of Islam. The Prophet of Islam himself forgave those who abused him and it is difficult to see how a law that prescribes a mandatory penalty of death for insulting him can be pronounced in his name.

Reciprocity

It is important to stress the question of reciprocity. I'm sure some people will ask why we should we be open and welcoming, while Christians in some Islamic countries don't even have the freedom to worship.

It is scandalous that that is so, but it has to be set against other situations in the Muslim world where Christians do have the freedom to worship, and that freedom is increasing in some countries. Sadly, in others it is being restricted and in yet others it is not allowed at all. I think, though, that we need to deal with each country as it is at a particular moment and not to tar them all with the same brush. Certainly within the international community, if Muslim nations are part of a regional grouping, as they may well be within the European Union, for example, then they will have to respect the rights of others just as everyone else does. But we need to be consistent. We cannot demand certain standards of poorer countries because we may have more power but not demand them of countries where we have less power and which are wealthier.

What about Christian mission to Islamic countries? Some people may see 'understanding my Muslim neighbour' as serving people in need.

Indeed, mission is an aspect of the Christian life and some people are called to engage in mission with different groups, some of which may be groups in Muslim countries. I can only say that a government minister in a Muslim country once said to me that there was a lot of pressure on him to restrict the numbers of foreign Christian missionaries in the country. To those who were exerting that pressure he replied, 'We send out Muslim missions to all parts of the world every year, to Africa, to Europe, to America – if we restrict them in coming here, don't you think that they will get wise to this sooner or later and restrict us from going there?' His argument was that the best way to promote Muslim international mission is to allow Christian international mission, and I agree with that.

Terrorism

Still the images of 11 September and the threat of further action live with us. Will this threat go away, do you think?

I think terrorism is here to stay. It will take different forms. In the last twenty years we have seen different kinds of terrorism. We are only just coming out of an era when terrorism was exercised in the name of an atheistic system, and as soon as atheistic communism collapsed in many parts of the world it was replaced by a chauvinistic nationalism, which often included religion as an aspect of it, sometimes in the form of Christianity. I'm thinking, in particular, of what happened in the Balkans. Terrorism has been influenced by religious and political ideas, it still is and it will continue to be. One form of terrorism which we must now expect is that influenced by a pathological and extremist version of Islam.

Where will the flashpoints be and how will it manifest itself?

First of all, I think the flashpoints, such as Israel–Palestine, Kashmir, Chechnya, Bosnia and Kosova, are the cause of it and not only the location for it, and it is very important to remember that. Some Muslims may certainly be moved to further extremist action because of the situation in the Holy Land. We cannot now expect that such action will take place only in the Holy Land. It may take place anywhere in the world. I think that is one of the lessons that 9/11 has taught us. The flashpoints are important because they illustrate the grievances that many Muslims have in relation to the West and in relation to the world community. There is a sense of injustice, and the sharper it is, the more extreme the measures to counter it will be.

Would you agree that 11 September changed the world for ever?

It has certainly changed the United States of America for ever! It has been seared into the consciousness of the American people and it will stay there for a very long time. It is partly because of the relative isolation of the United States from the rest of the world that attacks against the American people on American territory have not been all that frequent or recent. It was the deliberate and sophisticated nature of the attacks that took people aback. It was the arbitrariness of them, and the targeting of what was seen as a symbol of American economic success. 11 September was certainly a very great evil and it has alerted us to a network of international terrorism which needs to be checked, not just for the sake of the West or the United States but for the safety of people from Algeria to Indonesia.

At the same time as recognizing the enormity of 11 September, though, we have to place what happened in New York that day alongside the huge atrocities that have taken place in the last 100 years. There were the two World Wars, the Holocaust, the Stalinist purges, the genocide against the Armenian and Assyrian Christians of the Middle East, the huge loss of life at partition between India and Pakistan, the loss of life from hunger and disease, and the impact of the HIV virus. All these are evils that continue to afflict our world and we must combat them as much as international terrorism.

Is it possible to say that anything good has come out of 11 September?

It is possible to say that some good is coming from this terrible event. While it must be acknowledged as a very great evil, many countries and many international organizations have now become aware of a network of terrorism. Some of us have been warning the world about the existence of this network and what has given rise to it for twenty years, but the world was not listening because it did not really affect those with power. Now it has affected them, and so the world is listening, and I'm glad, for the sake of the powerless in Africa, Asia and Latin America, that the international community is now acting against this network. That the voice of moderate Islam is starting to be heard more clearly is another great good that's come out of 11 September. And that voice is heard not just in relation to non-Muslims but has also created a dynamic in Muslim countries that will lead to a greater respect for law and for freedoms in Muslim countries themselves.

What about the role of the media?

Generally speaking, the media have been very interested in the dramatic and the visible aspects of what has happened, but the more subtle developments – of dialogue between religious scholars which would have been impossible a few years ago, of some Muslim countries acting against terrorist movements on their soil, and of the scrutiny of the economic arrangements that affect terrorists – have received very little attention, even though they are developments of lasting importance.

Optimism or pessimism?

Finally, as we look to the future, are you optimistic that there will be more understanding, or pessimistic that there will be more polarization when it comes to 'understanding my Muslim neighbour'?

I feel there is a great desire on every side for more understanding, but there are some obstacles. In the West, the far right can certainly cause misunderstanding to grow. There is also a great danger of extremists in some Muslim countries refusing to allow the majority of the population to open up to the world. In Iran, for instance, there is a great desire by a vast majority of the people and, indeed, of the religious scholars to open up more to the world, but a small minority is preventing greater development in that particular country, and what can be said of Iran can also be said of other countries. The extent to which networks of terrorism are checked is also important, and, if only those networks that may actively threaten the West are checked, then, from my point of view, that is not enough. Many of these networks are actually a greater threat to indigenous populations and particularly to Christians. Here I'm thinking of some of the countries of Central Asia and also of a country like Indonesia. So there has to be some even-handedness about how these networks are dealt with and, if we have learnt any lesson, it must be that this is a network of movements and that they are all interconnected. If we leave one untouched, that has implications for others.

And in terms of people coming together, growing together as neighbours, how optimistic are you?

I have never found any difficulty in making friends with Muslims and getting on with my Muslim relatives. Many of my best friends, as they say, are Muslims ... and I hope and pray that there will be increased tolerance between neighbours. More than that, I hope that many, many Christians will actively devote themselves to 'understanding my Muslim neighbour'.

Glossary of Terms

Caliph. 'Successor' – originally to the Prophet of Islam. Ruler of Islam.

Dhimma. 'Responsibility' or 'protection'. In return for protection from Muslims, Jews and Christians in lands conquered by Islam paid special taxes but did not enjoy certain civic and political rights. They enjoyed a limited amount of religious liberty.

Haj (5th pillar of Islam). The pilgrimage to Mecca (the 'greater pilgrimage').

Ijtihad. Striving to relate the *shari^{c}a* to present circumstances.

Imam. The leader of the community. Shiite Muslims use *Imam* to denote a descendant of the prophet, who is their spiritual leader. In many parts of the world, the *Imam* leads the community in the mosque and provides for rites of passage, for instance, and leadership in prayer, for the maintenance of the mosque and so on.

Islam. 'Surrender' to God. Some Muslims also say it means 'peace'.

Jihad. From the root *'Jahada'* which simply means 'to strive', both in the personal sense of individual reform and in the sense of striving to make Islam acceptable and to promote its spread throughout the world. Some, however, interpret the repeated exhortations to fight those who oppose the way of Allah literally.

Madrassa. An Islamic religious school.

Mujahid. A fighter for Islam, both figuratively and literally.

Mushrikūn. Pagans – those who associate other gods with the one, true God.

Ramadan. The month of fasting.

Salat (2nd pillar of Islam). The ritual prayers which Muslims make five times each day.

Saum (4th pillar of Islam). The practice of fasting during the month of *Ramadan.*

Shahadah (1st pillar of Islam). The profession of belief that there is no God but Allah and that Muhammed is the Prophet or apostle of God.

Shariᶜa. Islamic law derived from the *Quran*, and guided by the six main collections of traditions about the Prophet of Islam.

Shiite. They belong to the Shīᶜat ʻAli, the Party of Ali. They believe that Ali, the Prophet of Islam's closest male relative, should have been his successor. They revere *imams* who are Ali's direct descendants, and they are the focus of personal authority through which, and by whom, the *Quran* and the traditions of the Prophet are interpreted for life today. Fewer than 20% of Muslims are *Shiites.*

Sunnah. The life, habits and religious practice of the Prophet of Islam, recorded by his family and companions.

Sunni. The branch of Islam which reveres the four 'rightly guided' caliphs, the companions and immediate successors of the Prophet of Islam. Today it focuses more on the authority of the *Quran* (and on how lawyers and theologians and scholars interpret that authority) than on a particular person. More than 80% of Muslims are *Sunnis.*

Sufi. The mystical tradition of *Sunni*, and to a lesser

extent, *Shiite*, Islam. *Sufis* are those who seek a close, direct and personal experience of God.

Sura. A chapter of the *Quran*, each of which is divided into *Ayahs*, or verses.

Ummah. The worldwide community of Islam.

ʿ*Umra.* The lesser pilgrimage.

Zakat (3rd pillar of Islam). Alms-giving – a word of Hebrew origin which is closely related to piety, so alms-giving arises out of piety.

Further Reading

Ahmed, Akbar S., *Living Islam*, BBC, 1993.

Akbar, M. J., *The Shade of Swords: Jihad and the conflict between Islam and Christianity*, Routledge, 2002.

Armstrong, Karen, *Islam, A Short History*, Phoenix Press, 2001.

Beverley, James A., *Understanding Islam*, Nelson, Nashville, 2001.

Blean, Jonathan and Blair, Sheila, *Islam: Empire of Faith*, BBC, 2001.

Bowker, John (ed.), *The Oxford Dictionary of World Religions*, Oxford University Press, 1999.

Cook, Michael, *The Koran*, Oxford University Press, 2000.

Davie, Grace, *Religion in Modern Europe*, Oxford University Press, 2000.

Gopin, Marc, *Holy War, Holy Peace – how religion*

can bring peace to the Middle East, Oxford University Press, 2002.

Gordon, Matthew S., *Understanding Islam*, Duncan Baird, 2002.

Gumley, Frances and Redhead, Brian, *The Pillars of Islam*, BBC, 1990.

Halliday, Fred, *Two Hours that Shook the World*, Saqi Books, 2002.

Ipgrave, Michael (ed.), *The Road Ahead – a Christian–Muslim Dialogue*, Church House Publishing, 2002.

Keene, Michael, *World Religions*, Lion, 2002.

Lewis, Philip, *Islamic Britain*, I. B. Tauris, 1994.

Markham, Ian (ed.), *A World Religious Reader*, Blackwell, 1996.

Nazir-Ali, Michael, *Islam, a Christian Perspective*, Paternoster, 1982.

——*Frontiers in Muslim–Christian Encounter*, Regnum, 1987.

——*The Roots of Islamic Tolerance*, Oxford Project for Peace Studies, 1990.

Rashid, Ahmed, *Jihad: the rise of militant Islam in Central Asia*, Yale University Press, 2002.

Ruthven, Malise, *Islam: A Very Short Introduction*, Oxford University Press, 2000.

Schimmel, Annemarie, *Islam: an Introduction*, State University of New York Press, 1992.

Smart, Ninian, *Background to The Long Search*, BBC, 1977.

Yusuf Ali, A, *Text, Translation and Commentary on the Holy Quran*, Islamic Foundation, Leicester, 1975.

A useful website can be found at: *www.bbc.co.uk/worldservice/people/features/world_religions*